PRIMER FOR GRAPHIC ARTS PROFITABILITY

A Money-Making Formula

PRIMER FOR GRAPHIC ARTS PROFITABILITY

A Money-Making Formula

by
Gary W. Millet
and
Ralph G. Rosenberg

△ **Millet Group, Inc.**
5012 Cliff Point Circle West
Colorado Springs, CO 80919

First Printing 1992
Second Printing 1993
Third Printing 1994

ISBN 1-881637-04-2

LCCN 92-061245

ORDER FORM: A mail order form for additional copies of this book and a video on the "Millet Triangle" is in the back of this book.

ATTENTION CORPORATIONS, COLLEGES, AND PROFESSIONAL ORGANIZATIONS: Quantity discounts are available on bulk purchases of this book for educational purposes or fund raising. Special books or book excerpts can also be created to fit specific needs. For information, please contact Millet Group, Inc., 5012 Cliff Point Circle West, Colorado Springs, CO 80919.

Preface

The purpose of this book is to provide a short, readable business and production primer aimed at refocusing graphic arts companies back to the basics. We want to clarify what seem to be complex issues and provide a day-to-day management tool to guide the growth of your company to profitability.

The graphic arts industry is characterized by a huge array of various size players ranging from the multi-billion dollar printers to the "Ma and Pa" photo studio. The one thing they all have in common, however, is they produce unique jobs and pages for their clients.

We have created 10 chapters to describe what we believe are the most significant aspects owners and managers must address in order to further the growth of their company's profits.

We would like to dedicate this book to our clients, those brave individuals who made that leap of faith in adopting our ideas and concepts and putting up with all of those implementation checklists. It has been extremely rewarding for us to see their profits improve and their companies prosper. In the final analysis, however, we think they are much happier than us because they got to keep the money.

In 1994 the Millet Group formed the *Institute for Graphic Arts Profitability*. This institute will conduct intensive workshops for graphic arts companies to assist them to increase their profitability.

Institute Mission Statement

"Train Chief Executive Officers, Controllers, Plant Managers, and Sales Managers of graphic arts companies to work as a team to develop and write a vision statement, growth plan, and implementation strategy using the interrelated principles of throughput, capacity, and profitability analysis."

Acknowledgments

The authors are most appreciative of the outstanding support we have received in producing *Primer for Graphic Arts Profitability*.

The excellent design and layout of the book cover and many of the charts was accomplished by Robin Cass, an Associate Technical Consultant in Scitex America Corporation's regional office in Los Angeles, California, headed by John Doe, Regional Manager.

The unique charts on productivity, overtime, and rework in the chapter on statistical process control were created by Pat Ternan, Director of Information Management, at Color Service in Seattle, Washington.

Joan Saucerman, owner of Word Broker in Colorado Springs, Colorado, produced the drafts and final text for us.

Abilene Paradox by Jerry Harvey provided food for thought for effective communications within a graphic arts company.

Without the support of Marilyn and Tom Ross, owners of About Books, Inc., in Buena Vista, Colorado, we would not have been able to publish this book within our short time lines. Using their expertise and frequent guidance, we were able to draft, edit, and publish this book in only five months from a standing start.

Table of Contents

Chapter 1

The Industry and Its Eroding Profits

Pretend some aliens from outer space have come to our favorite planet, Earth. They look like, talk like, and sometimes even act like us. Their mission is to commingle with earthlings in different industries and learn strategies and techniques used in each industry.

One evening on late night TV one of the aliens is watching a commercial for one of our seminars. The commercial says, "Come on down to You-Know-Where Hotel tomorrow for a free seminar on the wonderful opportunities in the graphics arts industry. Just make this call, 1-900-Graphic, and sign up for the free seminar on *How to Get Into the Graphic Arts Industry for No Money Down.*" The commercial looked so inviting the alien could not resist; he called to sign up.

At the seminar the next day, the alien was introduced into the graphics arts industry by learning a few interesting facts.

1. There is excess production capacity in the industry. Supply exceeds demand.

2. Prices are dropping quickly.

3. Technology is advancing at an alarming rate. The overall cost per unit of technology is dropping, but the turnover of technology is becoming more rapid. Thus, the overall cost of technology is not necessarily dropping.

4. Skilled labor is becoming scarce. Employers require more education and training to keep up with the rapid evolution of technology. There are very few good formal continuing education programs in existence. This scarcity in the skilled labor pool is driving the cost of labor up.

5. The growth of the overall industry is trending under four percent annually.

6. Tasks such as design, pre-press, and press, once performed by a variety of different companies, are rapidly becoming consolidated due to the new technology. This consolidation of tasks is leading to the breakdown of vertical production segments and essentially creating new companies that offer a much broader "full service" concept.

7. Material costs are dropping per job because of electronic production means, but are increasing because the size of the volume purchased is declining. This will have a tendency to drive up the price per unit.

8. Customers expect their jobs to be turned faster, usually within three days or less. This creates tremendous stress on companies to increase capacities or invest in technology that will allow a greater volume of work to be done in a shorter period of time.

9. Customers are becoming more and more involved with the production cycle. Many times the disks supplied by customers require tremendous work in order to get them into a condition called electronic ready art. Customers also play an important role in the timing of the production cycle as they often insist on reviewing the job during the production cycle. Their response often dictates the success or failure of the cycle.

10. Debt-to-equity ratios are increasing. There has been a decrease in overall industry income; thus, retained earnings and equity have decreased. This fact, coupled with the need to add new technology, has increased the debt-to-equity ratio overall.

11. The days sales outstanding (DSO) has increased. This is the measurement of how fast account receivables are being collected based on sales volume. There has been an increase of several days added to the cycle. This means that companies have become larger banks to their customers and cash flow has decreased.

In the past couple of years, many companies have gone out of business. The Northeast has been hit the hardest. This decrease of profits finds companies scrambling to find ways to hold profits steady and to combat profit shrinkage other than just adding new technology and hoping for the best. The remaining chapters contain some ideas and concepts that will enable a company to refocus and build some day-to-day management tools and provide a guide to profitability.

Chapter 2

The President and His Organization

Two general types of personalities, experiences, and interests will be used to describe the wide variety of corporate leadership within today's graphic arts industry. Each president, of course, is unique. However, we have found that these two contrasting blends of talents sharply influence the corporate culture.

Type one are the *tradesmen*. They have been in the business for 20 years or more. Now in their late forties to late fifties, or beyond, these presidents know the conventional graphic arts business very well. They may have started in the trade as a scanner operator, stripper, dot etcher, pressman, cameraman, etc. They are comfortable with the tried and true conventional methods of producing four-color work. Many also may have invested in electronic processes.

Type two are the *technologists*. They are younger, perhaps in their mid to late thirties. These presidents may or may not have grown up in the trade. They have studied technology, especially the emergence of desktop publishing with the Macintosh, and realize its impact on the marketplace. They seem to sense that the optimum solution for success is a mix of electronic process (desktop publishing), high-end electronic assembly workstations, and new high tech press and bindery equipment.

Where the tradesmen are still comfortable with the conventional process with some mix of electronic technology, the technologists want to do a great deal of their work electronically. They view strippers as remnants of a bygone era and they envision presses becoming highly robotic.

Of the various functions that challenge a president each day within the plant, the tradesmen's primary interest is on the production process, with sales as a secondary focus. The technologists' primary focus is converting technological capabilities to sales opportunities.

They both know good color when they see it. They know, like, and care for their people. They are friendly and easy to work with. However, only the technologists are comfortable with the computer revolution—not only with high-end systems but also desktop publishing. The technologists have personal computers in their offices and at home and use them daily. The tradesmen do not have PCs and are even unfamiliar with the keyboard.

Unfortunately, neither of these types of presidents have much experience or education in finance. The accountant prepared income statements and balance sheets are a bit of a mystery and they are seldom used to manage the company. Neither type of president has a business plan or even a sales forecast for the next few months.

These presidents, although of diverse backgrounds and experience, both sense the ongoing revolution in the industry, the changing needs of their current client base, and the fact that technology is exploding geometrically. They are, however, unable to quantify what impact these factors will have on the profitability of their business. They know the comfortable, profitable life of yesteryears will not be repeated unless changes are made. But what changes?

This uncertainty about the direction of the graphic arts industry is manifested in the organizational structure of the company. Just as there are two general types of presidents, there are two general types of organization. The first is characterized by the traditional line and block diagrams with lots of "managers." The second is best characterized by no organization at all. There may be titles for key individuals but job descriptions, responsibilities, and authority are ill defined in both models.

The lack of clear responsibilities usually is most apparent in production. The traditional "departments" of scanning, stripping, and proofing all have managers. As new technology was added, especially desktop and high-end electronic production equipment, more departments and more managers were added.

In one $3 million company we found seven managers, none with clear responsibilities. In a $15 million company we found 16 managers, all reporting to the president!

We have found that the younger employees, no matter what job they perform in the company, do not want a lot of organizational structure. They want an open communication system and to feel like an integral part of the team.

We believe the best organization chart is no chart at all. Instead the organization can be represented by a complete layout of the work flows, tracing the job from when it comes in the front door on a work order until it goes out the back door with an invoice. This system connotes a team approach and shows how each person, working in their functional area, contributes to the overall profitability of the company. (See Chapter 10, Managing the Process.)

Managers are needed, but there should be many more supervisors or "leads" than managers. In order to qualify for the title manager, a person should have a direct influence over people, money, equipment/materials, and products/ services. Anything less, and the person is a supervisor. *Supervisor* is a good title. *Lead* also is a good title. Both suggest a hands-on approach.

Management meetings seem a rarity in small- to mid-sized companies (under $6M) in the graphic arts industry. There are two primary reasons for this. First, without clear responsibilities for key personnel, it makes little sense to have weekly management meetings. Second, the tradesmen, and to a lesser extent the technologists, have not previously worked in large corporate environments. They believe, often erroneously, that they can run the company by the seat of their pants. They simply are uncomfortable with an organizational structure and thus shy away from weekly meetings.

This lack of structure creates an environment where upper management does not communicate well within itself. This, in turn, filters down to the supervisory level and eventually to all employees. The net result of this lack of communication is increased rework, lower productivity, higher overtime, and mediocre job quality.

Weekly management meetings are essential. They should be short (less than one hour), scheduled the same time each week, have an agenda announced in advance, and the minutes should be recorded. Attendance should be limited to the true managers in the company.

The one question that we are asked time and time again is, "What do other presidents in the industry do on a day-to-day basis?" To provide insight into this question, three model work days will be described. However, just as with the two personality types that were discussed earlier, no one president fits precisely one of these models.

In Model I, the president is sales driven. He actively manages the sales staff and spends over half of his time out of the office working with existing accounts and prospecting for new ones. This model fits many of the technologists, but few of the tradesmen.

In Model II, the president works mostly inside doing a little bit of everything all day long. His time is not managed, but more crisis driven. The tradesmen characterize this model the best.

In Model III the president is confused. He neither works outside in the sales area or gets involved with issues inside. He is overwhelmed by the changes in the industry and is not sure what to do so he tends to do nothing. Both the tradesmen and the technologists can fall into this rut, although neither will realize it or do so intentionally. An outside observer is needed to spot this management paralysis.

The key factors that have caused this confusion for the presidents and their staffs is the rapidly changing industry (see Chapter 1, The Industry and Its Eroding Profits). Without a clear vision of where they want to take the company in the next few years, or even worse, a vision without the commitment to make the changes, the presidents default to the status quo.

The status quo eventually leads to negative cash flow and increased debt. A downward cyclic spiral gradually gains momentum and becomes harder and harder to reverse. To avoid this cycle, all employees should be asked to participate in improving the company. The next chapter will describe a planning system that can increase communications and strengthen the overall management system.

Chapter 3

Front-End Planning

In many graphic arts companies job planning is done *during the production process*. The production (or manufacturing) manager often receives a fragmentary description of the job requirements and is told that it is a rush job. He rushes it through each department manager, from scanning to proofing, allowing each department to determine what they *think* the client wants.

The job is produced on time. The sales person shows it to the client. However, the client rejects the job and sends it back to "be done right." The cycle is repeated. Rework costs a fortune. The company loses money. Production workers are blamed for not doing it right the first time. Goodwill with a client is lost. Does this sound familiar?

Front-end planning is the management tool to reduce what is perceived as the single greatest problem in any graphic arts company—*the lack of communication*. This conclusion was reached after studying interdepartmental working groups in over a dozen companies. These groups consistently identified lack of communication as the key factor contributing to rework and late jobs.

Job planning is a front-end function. If done correctly, good planning will decrease production time by eliminating rework; optimum work flows will be selected *before* the job enters production; the client's technical and color specifications will be documented using easy-to-read instructions and graphics; and all personnel involved in the planning process will know the details of the job soon after it comes in the front door.

Questions or issues involving the job will be identified and resolved before the production process begins. An extra two hours in the front-end planning effort can save many hours or even days in production.

The net result of these positive outcomes can be a *dramatic increase in profitability*. Companies that have implemented and sustained this front-end process have increased income between 6 percent and 30 percent. In a $3 million company this translates to at least $180,000 in increased net income.

A chart outlining a typical front-end job planning system is shown. The concept can be applied to all companies. The specific functions, however, will vary.

A good front-end planning process begins with a work order completed by the *sales person*. It is the sales person who has the best idea what the client wants. Verbally passing this information on to a Customer Service Representative (CSR) is not enough. CSRs are too busy to be sales secretaries! It is our experience that the work order must be filled out in detail as step one in the job process.

TYPICAL FRONT END JOB PLANNING SYSTEM

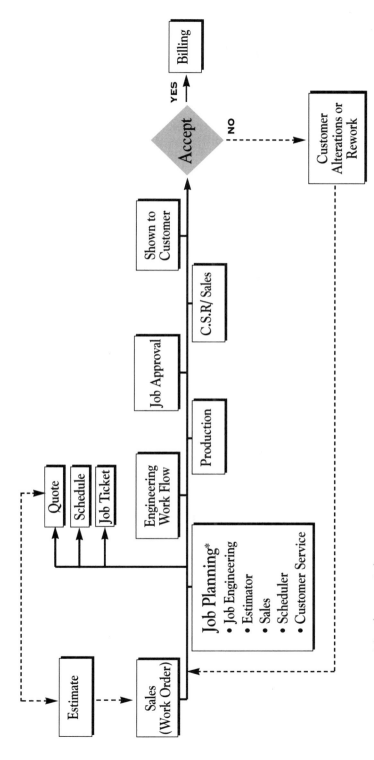

* Attendees as required

The quarterback of the front-end planning process is the *Job Engineer*. He or she is an expert on all facets of production—especially on high-end electronic system operations, the use of desktop publishing equipment such as the Macintosh, and the latest press and bindery. The Job Engineer carefully goes over the work order with the sales person, if possible. A *huddle* is then called by the Job Engineer who serves as the planning quarterback. The key players receiving instructions in the huddle will vary by job, but they could include all of the following individuals— CSR, sales person, scheduler, estimator, and production manager.

Some managers argue that they do not have time for the huddle. Yes, the huddle takes time. Perhaps 10 minutes or so. However, the profitability touchdown that can be achieved pays for this small amount of time many times over.

The Job Engineer determines how the job will flow through the plant to meet technical requirements, the client-imposed delivery date, *and* optimize plant capacity. A job engineering work flow document is then prepared with simple, easy-to-understand written and graphical instructions documenting the flow of the job through each department or functional process area in the plant.

This work flow document should show production functions in the order they must be performed. It may be necessary to perform actions in serial or in sequence (*e.g.*, stripping-contacting-proofing-press-bindery). When possible, however, actions should be performed in parallel (scan transparencies to an electronic workstation; process a client prepared line work diskette through the Macintosh to the electronic workstation.) Many more pre-press functions run in parallel than press functions.

Closely tied to job engineering is scheduling. Ideally the Job Engineer and Scheduler should sit side by side. The *Scheduler* knows where every job is in the plant and when each action will be completed, by department. Through a graphical display of this information, departments with over and under capacity will be readily apparent as the schedule is updated, preferably four times a day or more. The Job Engineer uses the scheduling information to pick the optimum work flow to avoid bottlenecks and use excess capacity, if available. The Scheduler, in turn, updates the schedule and then displays new capacities.

The Job Engineer work flow document, coupled with the schedule, sets the stage for the CSR to create the job ticket, either manually or automated, and enter the job in production. The CSR now becomes the information conduit for the job—keeping the client and sales person informed as to the status of the job. If new information is obtained, the CSR then provides it to the Job Engineer so the process can be updated.

At the same time the job ticket is being created, the *Estimator* can finalize the estimate and turn it into a quote. In many cases, the job will have been estimated before the work order was prepared. In this case, the Estimator will validate the estimate to determine if the job has changed, causing a price change. The quote is documented and will be the basis for billing the job, provided there are no customer alterations.

These front-end planning functions should be performed for all jobs and in all size companies. For simple jobs, such as loose scans only, the job engineering process can be done very quickly. In small companies, one individual may wear more than one hat. The Job Engineer may also be the Scheduler, for example.

The Production (or Manufacturing) Manager's job is to *get the job done* on time and to the highest standards of quality. The Production Manager holds a "line" position in the company. He should control all aspects of production, both conventional and electronic, and establish quality control as part of the production process. (See Chapter 10, Managing the Process.)

Once the job is produced, it must be approved before leaving the plant. Approval authority must be established and enforced or jobs will be shown to clients before they are approved internally. Although job and color approval occurs at the end of the production process, we have included it in this chapter because it "closes the loop" on the job planning process.

Job approval is a two-tier process. Tier I approval is done by the production manager to insure that all aspects of the job have been completed as specified by the Job Engineer. Tier II approval involves judging color. This is a subjective area and what may be pleasing to one client is not to the other. Very few people in a plant have an expert eye for color.

The selection of the color approval authority is an important decision. It can be anyone in the plant. The key point is to establish firm policies for who approves color.

A well-integrated front-end planning process will sharply reduce production costs, increase customer satisfaction, and, of course, improve company profitability. Yet just establishing a good front-end planning process is not enough. It must be made to work, day in and day out.

Changing a process is one thing. Implementing the change is quite another. Time after time employees state that changes in the process will not last because management lacks commitment. Strange as it may seem, the employees often have more commitment to improving profitability than the owners and managers. They know that profitability means secure jobs.

The key to sustaining the planning process is obtaining a long-term (*e.g.*, three-year) commitment from upper management and getting everyone involved every week. Processes take root in a company when all employees feel part of a team and are convinced the policies and procedures are in the best interest of the company. Employees *want the company to be profitable.*

Weekly meetings are a must and a three-month period should be allowed to implement a good front-end planning process. To sustain the process, twice monthly or, as a minimum, monthly meetings are essential. These meetings should focus on never ending quality improvements.

No process is static. The market changes. Technology changes. People change. The front-end process must evolve and constantly be fine-tuned to optimize the resources within the plant and increase profits.

Finally, the effects of the front-end process on reducing rework, increasing productivity, and decreasing overtime must be measured statistically. (See Chapter 7, Statistical Process Control.)

Chapter 4

Production STUFF and Throughput

Everyone knows them. They are out there and they are growing in numbers. Yes, they are the *technonerds*. These are the people who love new technology and cannot for the life of them understand why every company has not rushed out and purchased the latest and greatest technology to make it available for their use.

The graphic arts industry has tried this approach for the last several years; it has not worked. All the new STUFF has not dramatically improved the overall net income of the industry. Many other industries are going through the same transformation with new equipment acquisitions and it has resulted in the same frustrations. The problem with STUFF is not the STUFF; it is the use of the STUFF. Throughput is the key.

Throughput is defined as the total number of sellable, completed, and delivered jobs that the production work flow is capable of producing in a given period of time. A *bottleneck* is defined as the operation(s) that is the inhibitor to additional needed throughput.

To describe throughput we will use the bucket theory, illustrated by the sketch. It shows a long pipe which represents the production capability of the company in terms of getting jobs through the plant to meet the demands of customers. The two main factors that determine the flow of jobs through the pipes are: (1) the diameter of the pipe (capacity), and (2) the speed in which the jobs flow through the pipe (pressure).

The following scenario illustrates the bucket theory and why the analysis of throughput is so very important for a company to maximize its potential profitability.

Bob owns a water company and supplies water to different communities in the rural areas. Bob has built a reservoir from which he draws the water through a 50 inch piping system and then delivers it to customers through a series of central canals. Bob has the opportunity to increase his water sales by 50 percent. In order to meet this new demand, Bob will need to expand his ability to supply the additional water needed. Bob has several choices:

1. Add a new 25 inch pipe

2. Add a new 50 inch pipe

3. Add a new pump to the existing 50 inch pipe

4. Add a new 25 inch pipe with a pump

What should Bob do?

Bob should analyze his alternatives for profitability and performance. This means he needs to look at throughput. He needs to figure out how much throughput he is currently getting and how much money the current throughput is making. Bob does not want to choose any alternative that will decrease his profits from current levels.

Ways To Increase Jobs in Bucket

1. Add another pipe
2. Increase pressure through pipe

Pipe Size = Manufacturing Capacity
Bucket Size = Market Demand

Job Manufacturing Process

JOB FLOW JOB FLOW JOB FLOW

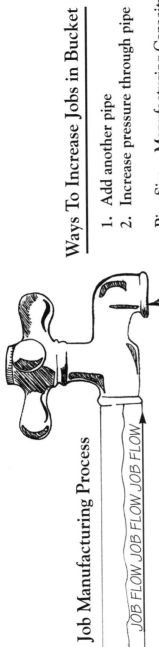

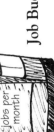

Job Bucket

Performing analysis is very similar to planning a trip. Whenever the question, "What is the most important thing to know when you are going to take a trip?" is asked, a myriad of answers occur. The most common answer is, "Where you are going."

This is not the right answer.

The most important thing a person needs to know when he is going to take a trip is,

"Where am I."

A person cannot get anywhere unless they know where they are.

Bob needs to find out where he is. The first part of the illustrated example is devoted to getting to know where Bob is and it is answered on the line titled "Current Demand," $175,200.

The next significant question in the analysis is to determine where Bob is going. He has one major objective—maximum profitability when meeting a demand of $280,320. The analysis will determine the best alternative.

The answer for Bob is to simply install an additional 25 inch pipe. The cost per cubic foot of water is highest with this alternative ($8.56/cubic foot), however, the profits are also the highest ($1,792,000). Cost can only be properly evaluated when it is done in relation to profit. Productivity must be increased in the bottleneck area in order to increase profits.

Although the cost per cubic foot of water is lowest when the pump alternative is selected ($6.62/cubic foot), installing a pump on his current 50 inch pipe is ineffective because it does not give Bob enough extra capacity (only 219,000 cubic feet). Remember margin percentage is not profit dollars.

Bob's Water Company
Throughput Analysis

Resource Name	Cubic Feet Per Hour	Cost of Resource	Cost to Install	Total Cost	Pipe Life in Hours	Cost Per Cubic Foot	Total Cap Cubic Foot
25 Inch pipe	5.00	600,000	150,000	750,000	17,520	8.56	87,600
50 Inch pipe	10.00	1,250,000	150,000	1,400,000	17,520	7.99	175,200
Pump for pipes	2.50	250,000	40,000	290,000	17,520	6.62	43,800

	Total Capacity	Capacity Demand	Price Per Cubic Foot	Total Revenue	Total Cost	Total Profit	
Current Demand	175,200	175,200	15	2,628,000	1,400,000	1,228,000	
New Demand		280,320	15	4,204,800	Max Demand		
with new 50" pipe	350,400	280,320		4,204,800	2,800,000	1,404,800	
with new pump	219,000	280,320		3,285,000	1,690,00	1,595,000	
with new 25" pipe	262,800	280,320		3,942,000	2,150,000	1,792,000	
with new 25" & pump	306,600	280,320		4,204,800	2,440,000	1,764,800	

Installing a 25 inch pipe and a pump creates excess capacity (306,600 cubic feet), however, not as much as a new 50 inch pipe (350,400 cubic feet). This would be the next best alternative should there be a 10 to 15 percent additional increase in demand.

Bob's problem in this illustration is rather simple. In a graphic arts company problems are more complex, the alternatives more numerous, and the information is harder to collect. Does this mean a company cannot apply the bucket theory? On the contrary, the bucket theory is even more important when the variables are greater and profit (or loss) is a reality. Those companies that analyze throughput, and the variables governing throughput, will make more effective decisions. If they act on those decisions, they will make more money.

Throughput governs the acquisition of STUFF. New equipment only should be acquired to solve a bottleneck. A dollar invested in acquiring STUFF for a non-bottleneck operation usually is a waste of a dollar. Productivity can help the company define what is the "best STUFF" to acquire because it measures the amount of output for a given amount of input.

When the cost of the STUFF is coupled with the additional revenues the increased throughput of jobs will bring, the result is *profit on STUFF*, closely related to *return on investment*.

People often ask, "What about STUFF acquired to do R&D for new processes or new work flows?" Our recommendation usually is to calculate the cost of the STUFF and then go to the sales vice president and tell him if this STUFF is needed for R&D his sales group will need to produce "X" dollars of sales to produce enough profits to pay for the STUFF. Otherwise, profits will simply decrease.

The most important equipment acquisition issue centers on deciding what is the right STUFF. To accomplish this, an overall *growth model* should be developed for the company (see Chapter 6, A Growth Model). A Growth Model is essentially an all inclusive macro plan for sales, production, and support. It details the sales mix, throughput and capacity, production costs, and support costs, and then puts everything into a money-making formula (see Chapter 9, The Money-Making Formula). This results in a very comprehensive interactive budget keyed to profits that is simple to use and one that everyone can understand.

Once the growth model is completed the company can break each segment apart into what are called micro plans. A *micro plan* is really the checklist, both quantitative and qualitative, for accomplishing the different segments of the growth plan. For instance, the section on *sales mix* in the growth plan will "roll out" into a sales plan. The *sales plan* will dictate what is projected to be sold by product classification and the *production plan* will result in showing what resources will be needed to support the sales plan. From the production plan comes the *resource acquisition plan* for STUFF.

Once this is established, the technical people know the budget and know what kind and level of throughput is needed from the STUFF. The hunt begins. The best way to ultimately decide whether the STUFF meets the throughput need is to test it. This is called a *benchmark*.

In the past, our industry has gotten away with the so-called "demo." Demos are not bad if the technical people are looking for an overview of the STUFF and to qualify the STUFF. Once the STUFF has been qualified it is time to move on to a detailed analysis.

A lot of STUFF is bought piecemeal. Some of this STUFF, some of that STUFF, but in the end none of the STUFF works well as a system because there are a lot of bottlenecks. STUFF needs to be purchased as a system of STUFF. This mind set needs to take place in the beginning and be driven by what the company really wants to produce to meet identified needs. It is usually a mistake to buy STUFF and then try to figure out who needs the products the STUFF makes. It will decrease profit.

Companies should buy STUFF as a system or a piece of an expanding system. Stand alone components usually are more expensive because they may reduce throughput.

A benchmark test can be used to confirm the STUFF being purchased "fits" the throughput needs and will integrate into the "system" in which the company produces work. Benchmarks test system throughput and confirm or deny capabilities in the sales literature. (All STUFF usually reads better than it lives.)

To do an effective benchmark, the vendor should be requested to set up a configuration and a simulated working production environment with the STUFF being considered for purchase. Also, the existing configuration can be tracked to establish a benchmark for comparison purposes. The system should be run by the exact number of people the vendor is proposing can run the system effectively. The reason for this is that labor is more expensive per hour than STUFF, and the easiest way to lose profit is to not do a labor cost analysis along with the cost analysis of the equipment acquisition.

Once the system has been set up properly, consider using the steps described below. They illustrate why benchmarks prove to be the "acid" test for STUFF.

1. The test should consist of more than one page and it should be typical. A typical job does not mean an average job; it means the composite of a job that includes the elements the company encounters on a day-to-day basis.

2. The test job must be done in its entirety including the planning and production of the end product. Record all downtime if there are equipment problems on the lapse time measurement and track the exact time for each function. Make every attempt to emulate the live production environment including alteration cycles (if required).

3. The results must be evaluated for quality and correctness. A quality checklist should be completed prior to going to the benchmark. Two people from the company should judge the quality independently and then aggregate their results.

4. The information from the benchmark will need to be validated for accuracy and completeness. A list of equipment used to perform the benchmark along with its original costs, maintenance, installation costs, and interest costs will need to be supplied.

5. The benchmark must be tracked accurately for labor time, machine time, and materials as well as total lapse time.

After the benchmark has been completed a return on investment (ROI) analysis should be undertaken to make sure this STUFF can increase profits.

Finally, there will always be new STUFF. Technology is increasing by leaps and bounds. The important thing to keep in mind is that new equipment technology is just STUFF and acquiring STUFF is not as important as using STUFF. If the company cannot use the STUFF to fix a defined bottleneck, profits probably will not increase. The end result is the company has more STUFF and it's not the right $$$STUFF$$$.

Chapter 5

Direct Costing and Labor

There are many different costing methods from which to choose. The choice of a costing system needs to be made carefully. The basis of selection should be the intended creation and use of the information that the costing system will produce. Although most people think costing has its roots in accounting, costing actually has its roots in microeconomics. The fundamental choice of a costing system will often determine how a company views itself in relation to its markets and how business will be conducted internally. What this really means is that the correct choice of a costing system can help make the company more money.

Direct costing is oriented toward the production of management information. The main reason why companies convert to direct costing is to achieve a more readable and consistent financial system that compares in some way to their operational systems. In the case of direct costing, this is achieved by being able to compare the direct margin on the financial statement to the direct margin on the sales margin reports and the work in process reports.

Once the credibility between the financial statements and the sales margin reports and work in process reports is established, management can start to rely on the operating documents to provide a reasonable indicator of the company's actual performance.

In a company using direct costing, the direct margin is the key indicator of performance. This margin percentage is the representation of how much resource is required to produce revenue dollars. Direct costs are always variable costs. They are the costs that are directly attributable and trackable to a specific job. While a job may require variable indirect costs, these costs cannot be reasonably tracked and, therefore, cannot be considered direct.

Direct costing allows for the disassociation of volume fluctuations from direct margin results. The reason this is accomplished is that the rates used in the direct costs are not *loaded costs*, meaning there are no fixed overhead costs allocated to the direct cost rate.

Fixed cost allocations in a full absorption system are volume dependent because they have been *absorbed* into the cost rates of production based on some preconceived volume level. The problem this presents is that jobs produced today cannot be compared directly with a job produced two years ago, a month ago, or two years from now, because the amount of overhead that is absorbed into the rates has changed dramatically over the years.

The second main reason, and the big advantage to direct costing, is in strategic price modeling and management of product pricing mix. Direct costing allows the pricing committee, estimator, sales manager, or whoever is responsible for pricing the ability to be more pro-active and precise in determining the correct pricing in order to gain a competitive advantage. Never forget the company is fighting a war out there and great weapons always come in handy.

Direct costing allows for the creation of *strategic pricing points*. These strategic pricing points can be determined quickly and without much effort. The main strategic pricing points are presented below and shown graphically in the chart.

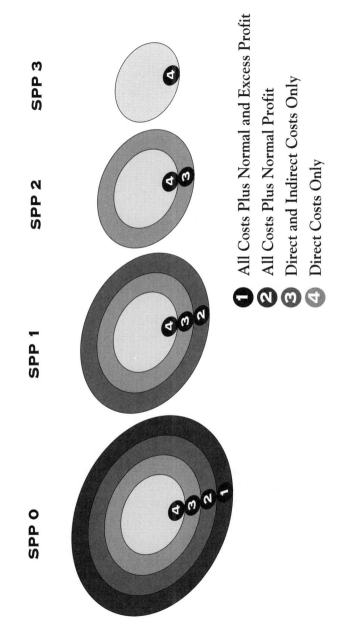

STRATEGIC PRICING POINTS

SPP 0   **SPP 1**   **SPP 2**   **SPP 3**

1. All Costs Plus Normal and Excess Profit
2. All Costs Plus Normal Profit
3. Direct and Indirect Costs Only
4. Direct Costs Only

SPP 0 The Oversell Price

The *oversell price* represents any price over the normal price (SPP 1). The difference between SPP 0 and SPP 1 directly contributes "net profit" dollars if SPP 0 was not used in price mix budgeting. Many sales compensation plans have special commission structures for compensating sales people for using oversell pricing.

SPP 1 The Normal Price

The *normal price* is determined by taking the direct costs and dividing them by one minus the *direct margin percentage*. This will produce the normal selling price. This price is to be used during normal operating times when the capacity of the plant is normal to high. It is also used in forecasting and the cornerstone in the stochastic pricing model. If impacted by actual job volume mix, it would build the forecasted direct costing section of the income statement.

SPP 2 The Contribution Price

The *contribution price* is determined by taking the direct costs and dividing them by one minus the *contribution margin percentage*. This means the price will be reduced to a level that only direct and indirect costs of production are covered. This price will not contribute to covering the costs of other selling and administrative expenses. This price is to be used when competition is keen, where there is excess plant capacity, and when the securing of the job will lead to securing future jobs with the opportunity to recapture lost profits.

SPP 3 The Drop Dead Price

The *drop dead price* is determined by isolating just the direct costs that will impact out-of-pocket expenditures and dividing this cost by one minus the *direct margin percentage.* No sunk variable costs should be used to compute the cost of production. The drop dead price is to be used when desperation becomes a corporate strategy. This price needs to be held as a last resort type of pricing. It is meant to secure volume when capacity is extremely low, or in "buying" a customer that promises to be a long-term investment for the company.

It is important to understand that a company has a different break-even volume requirement at different pricing points. *Break-even volume* is calculated by using the normal price computation and spreading the direct margin over the indirect production and noncommission selling and administrative overheads. To think that every job will be sold at the normal price (SPP 1) is not realistic. Therefore, price mix management is essential to using direct costing as a pricing tool.

Price mix management is done by developing a process that statistically tracks pricing level changes (any price other than the normal price) and relates those changes to plant capacity and other market statistics. The opportunity to improve market segment choice lies in the company's ability to identify and analyze those relationships that directly or inversely correlate pricing to plant capacity or other internal or external factors.

The most important goal in price mix management is maintaining homeostasis in the pricing model. Large swings in pricing may ultimately compute to the average normal price, but it also substantially increases the risk of not meeting the average normal price (SPP 1) when product mix fluctuates. Establishing an acceptable pricing zone is recommended to help in the management of the pricing process.

A good practical way to micro manage pricing is to develop a pricing board. The *pricing board* is a board mounted in the estimating area or the sales manager's office where the four pricing populations (SPP 0 through SPP 3) have been outlined. Each estimate is displayed on the board under the appropriate pricing zone. This establishes a running total of both estimates by volume and relative margin, and gives the sales manager a constant update of where he is for the month on both volume and margin.

There should also be a section on the pricing board for actual jobs won that month doing the same thing. Some computer systems have the ability to produce these statistics, but a board provides a much better visual overview of the situation and actually presents the case that it has to be managed in order to be updated. The big attraction for full absorption in the past was that it required little management because everything was thrown into one inclusive rate. To a knowledgeable sales manager it is almost an insult.

We believe most companies, after performing the suggested analyses, will find that direct costing is best, at least for graphic arts.

And now for labor. Many people think graphic arts is a capital intensive industry. They have been focused on the purchasing of capital equipment, from large web presses costing $6,000,000 to buying new Mac's with the latest and most sophisticated software. The analyses in this book repeatedly document that the graphic arts industry is labor, not capital, intensive.

To verify if this is true in a company, it is necessary to review the income statement and add up all the depreciation from equipment plus the repairs and maintenance for the year and divide it by the total sales. If the company is a full web printer, the total should be less than 4 percent, if it is a full electronic color house, the total should be below

11 percent. If the company is a mixture of sheet-fed, color, and web, the total should be somewhere in between.

Now do the same thing for all the production and production support labor and benefits. Which is higher? Labor almost always will be higher. It is going to be somewhere in the 14 percent to 22 percent range for a printer and somewhere between 18 percent and 33 percent for a pre-press trade shop. In almost all cases, labor exceeds the cost of machines.

If a company stops here, this little exercise does not pass the "So What Test." The importance of knowing whether the industry is labor or capital intensive is that it provides the basis of where strategies have the biggest potential to increase profitability.

The reason the industry seems to be capital intensive is that so much focus is paid to tools of the job. From a technical standpoint the debt-to-equity ratios are also high, indicating a capital intensive industry. The high debt-to-equity ratios are deceiving. The real reason for high debt-to-equity ratios is the low equity, not the high debt. Many companies in the industry are owner-operated and the equity sections are often manipulated due to tax strategies.

A company needs to be concerned about the labor intensiveness, because the acquisition of additional tools or other resources must generally be oriented towards the leveraging of labor. This means that purchasing other resources for production should be planned around a reduction of labor at a ratio higher than the cost to acquire the resource necessary to reduce the labor. This general plan will add profits and reduce risk.

Most companies do not devote much time or effort to the analysis and micro management of their labor. Labor is always added more casually than equipment and without much analysis on its impact. This lack of attention can drive the costs of a company up quickly and dramatically. Very few companies respond by immediate reduction even when it is dictated.

There are many companies not large enough to support the cost of a full-time human resource department. Specific tasks such as employee search, hiring/firing practices, performance evaluation, training, and so forth, are not done with the precision they need to be in order to optimize the use of the labor and increase productivity. This will become a major issue from now on and companies need to look into finding some type of support for this area in order to optimize their labor force. (See Chapter 7 for techniques of quantifying the impact of labor.)

Here are some general suggestions for micro managing the labor issues at your company:

1. Compute the ratio of people to sales and profits for the following major areas: executives/owners, sales, sales support, production, production support, and administration. Management for the company is located in the executive/owners, sales support, production support, and administration. This number should "roll up" into the overall percentage of labor to sales and be plotted monthly or when any new people are added to the payroll.

2. In order for a new person to be added to the payroll, an analysis will be needed to show how the person will impact profits through using the Money-Making Formula described in Chapter 9.

3. Any acquisition of a resource should have a section describing its impact on the labor. In many cases the decrease of labor will be the justification for the addition of the equipment.

4. Do away with organization charts. These charts are not representative of the actual deployment of labor nor do they define the actual communication channels and are generally dysfunctional. Instead, perform a general work

flow analysis by area and indicate where the people are needed to optimize the work flow. This is essential to improving work flow, describing the job for which the person is going to be held accountable, and establishing the proper channels for communication.

5. Acquiring people is no different than acquiring equipment. A person must be added only when curing a bottleneck area. Many personnel acquisitions are made on an emotional basis, not an economic basis. The same rules of throughput apply to labor as well as to capital equipment.

Companies that effectively lever their labor are generally more profitable. It is often the key issue we address when evaluating a company's position in reference to the industry. It also offers the best opportunity to improve profits quickly.

The most difficult thing to do is decrease a work force. Even when a company knows it needs to do it, it has a tendency to think it can relocate people into some other area and not have to actually deal with the problem. This type of thinking generally results in loss of profit and puts the entire company at risk. It is much better to face the reality, make the decision, get it over with, and move on.

When dealing with labor issues it is easy to fall into the trap that the needs of the few outweigh the needs of the many. The real axiom a company wants to focus on is the needs of the many outweigh the needs of the few. Good luck with this one; it is tough.

Chapter 6

A Growth Model

A single financial tool defined here as the Growth Model is most helpful in managing the month-to-month operations of a graphic arts company. Somehow the traditional *income statement* and *balance sheet* remain a mystery to many presidents. Perhaps the main reason for this is that neither document, in itself, provides a complete snapshot of how the company is doing.

The income statement often is the most misleading. If the company has heavy debt, as many do nowadays as a result of declining profits, the principal payments on the debt may be well in excess of the allowable depreciation. Also, if the company is behind on payments to suppliers, this fact may not be apparent on the income statement.

In theory, the depreciation claimed on the income statement should almost equal the principal payments that reduce liabilities on the balance sheet. However, in many cases the extra heavy debt load overrides this theory.

The cash flow projection, is the most useful. However, it is rarely prepared by the controller or accountant. They need sales and margins to complete the cash flow projections and sales managers (or the presidents) seldom prepare these. The absence of a cash flow projection, coupled with the complexities of the income and balance sheet, create a situation where the management team seldom knows where they are on finances, especially if they are operating in the red.

Our approach to this problem is the *Growth Model*. It integrates and projects *all* aspects of the company operations into a single, easy-to-understand spreadsheet. The president and his upper management team can easily use it to perform "what if analysis." It is similar to a cash flow projection, but provides a more complete description of the source of sales revenues and variable production expenses based on volume.

If the projected increase in sales exceeds the plant capacity, then resources (people and equipment) are added one at a time to meet the production demand. Through this approach, bottlenecks are identified and eliminated through the judicial addition of resources. (See Chapter 4, Production STUFF.)

The Growth Model combines data from the sales projection, income statement, and balance sheet. All input is constructed as a variable so that the change in any revenue or cost item has an immediate impact on net income and monthly cash flow. Shown on the next page are the major categories that can be used to construct a Growth Model.

The management team, including the president, has a far easier time understanding where it is and where it is going by examining a single document with bottom line numbers.

Once approved, the Growth Model must be updated monthly, or even more often. It becomes the tool to project where the company will be in the months ahead. The entire management team can use the Growth Model.

Constructing A Growth Model

FUNCTIONAL AREA	DESCRIPTION
PROJECTION OF INCOME	
Gross Sales	Projected by market niche, by sales person, for each month out 12-18 months.
Direct Costs	For labor, materials, machine (depreciation), buyouts, and sales commissions. These are increased in direct portion to the sales effort and can be by department, or even by individual in a small company. (See Chapter 5, Direct Costing and Labor.)
Indirect Costs	For labor, such as customer service, materials and machines, not directly related to producing a job. These also should be tied to job volume but not on a linear basis.
Selling Expenses	For sales and marketing expenses, to include draws for the sales personnel. Tie to the sales projections.
General and Administrative Expenses	All other expenses, most of which are fixed or semi-fixed.
Total Operating Expenses	(Sales less direct, indirect, selling, and General/Administration expenses.)

Interest Expenses	For all debt payments, to include line of credit.
Net Income (pre-tax)	Subtract interest expenses from operating expenses.

CONVERSION TO CASH FLOW

Opening Cash Balance	From the checkbook.
Plus Net Income	From net income (above).
Plus Machine Costs	From direct and indirect costs plus any depreciation included in General/Administration expenses.
Plus Principal Payments	From the balance sheet.
Plus New Acquisitions	If new acquisitions are anticipated, list total out of pocket expenses by month.
Monthly Cash Flow	Addition of the above (opening balance excluded).
Ending Cash Balance	Opening cash plus monthly cash flow. (This will be either a positive or negative number.)

In the finance area, it is critical to be able to project cash flow, especially for those companies that are on cyclic sales cycles. For example, high sales months may be in the spring and fall while the summer months are slower and early winter is the most difficult period. If this cycle is prevalent, operating expenses should be reduced to coincide with the lag in cash. Conversely, the sales staff should make every attempt to build business during the normally low periods.

The *Production Manager* also is a key user of the Growth Model. Requirements for the addition of production resources (labor and machines) can be predicted by the Growth Model. Addition of new resources should be aimed at the projected bottleneck. (See Chapter 4, Production STUFF.) Various shift alternatives can also be analyzed in the model to optimize productivity, work flow, and profitability.

Like the Production Manager, the *Sales Manager* can also be a frequent user of the Growth Model. He or she should have each sales person project their sales by market niche, by account, and by month. This data not only can be very useful to manage the sales process, but it is essential for projecting the cash flow cycle.

The more managers that share in building and using the Growth Model, the better. Sharing of company information, like the Growth Model, helps build company dedication and commitment.

Chapter 7

Statistical Process Control: Applying the So What Test

Even the term *statistical process control* (or SPC) is a bit overwhelming to most people in almost any industry, but especially in the graphic arts industry. In any profession there is a mix of "left side" brain people who are good at the sciences, to include statistics, and "right side" brain people who are more comfortable with the arts and social sciences.

The graphic arts industry is dominated by the right side brainers. This creates a difficult challenge for the management information system (MIS) specialist who has the staff responsibility for collecting, analyzing, and displaying key information.

Most automated companies have a wealth of data residing in the computer. Mountains of reports are spit out by the machine every month or so. This deluge of data often is dropped on the president's desk without analysis, and the MIS/accounting staff can now say to themselves that they have informed the boss. Nothing could be further from the truth.

The president, often the head right side brainer, politely accepts the data, leaves it on his desk for a couple of days, and (when no one is looking and the janitor is due that night) throws it in the garbage can.

Presidents want analyzed data keyed to their needs. Data, in itself, is not enough. The goal is to produce a refined product—an *intelligence report*. (Raw information can always be provided later.)

The intelligence report must pass the *So What Test*. This test is very simple. It is based on this premise: "So what if I get the information? Can I use it? Will I use it?" If the answer is no to either question, the information does not pass the So What Test.

There are three quantifiable activities in the graphic arts industry that lend themselves to statistical process control. These are *productivity*, *overtime*, and *rework*. If the status of each of these is measured and reported in an easy-to-understand format, direct costs can be controlled and profit per job can increase. (See Chapter 5, Direct Costing and Labor.)

Productivity is the first factor that lends itself to statistical process control. Productivity is defined using the following three variables.

1. Total Regular and Overtime Hours Worked

2. Total Hours Working on Billable Jobs

3. Total Hours Doing Rework (Not Customer Alterations)

The first variable, total regular and overtime hours worked, is easy to measure and readily available in most graphic arts companies that use either a manual or automated payroll system.

Total time working on a billable job, the second variable, often is much more difficult to document. Many companies do not have a direct costing system nor do they record employee time by job, separated from machine time. Thus, they do not know if a specific job is profitable. Without this information, pricing is, at best, a crap shoot.

For those companies that are tracking direct labor per job, it is essential that the MIS person stress to all employees the importance of accurately logging on and off jobs. The weekly data must be verified often. Total hours on billable work, for instance, cannot exceed total hours worked. Department managers or supervisors who do not work directly on jobs all of the time should be accounted for separately as indirect costs or the data will be skewed.

The third variable, hours of rework, is particularly difficult to document because many production workers do not know if they are doing original, alterations, or rework. They are simply doing their job. It is important that the Management Information Specialist, Job Engineer, and Production Manager devise a system to identify these three types of work.

To address this problem analytically, charts can be developed to display the productivity levels with and without rework. This is important because productivity has two different meanings in a company. To the president, rework clearly is not productive because he or she is not being paid by the client. However, to the production worker, he may be doing rework because it is required. In short, the worker views himself as productive because in many cases he or she has no control over rework.

Productivity only can be calculated when accurate statistics are available to measure each of these variables. A formula that can be used for calculating productivity is shown below. It assumes rework hours can be documented.

If this cannot be done accurately, then drop rework hours from the equation and just use billable time divided by total hours worked.

Total Hours Worked on Billable Jobs
Minus
Total Hours Doing Rework
Divided By
Total Regular and Overtime Hours

The above formula should be used to calculate productivity for each department directly involved in producing jobs. Once the data is compiled it can be loaded into a spreadsheet, such as Lotus 1-2-3, and graphed. The chart entitled Percentage of Productive Hours Worked by Area is an example of how productivity data can be graphed by department.

The second important set of statistics that needs to be collected and analyzed is overtime. In studies of a number of companies, often overtime receives little analytical attention from the President, Controller, and Production Manager. When asked, the Controller will usually state, "I have informed the president on this problem and I am very concerned." However, often this data is buried in the 10-12 page data dump described earlier.

Like productivity data, the overtime data should be entered in a spreadsheet and graphed by department. This information then can be displayed graphically, side by side with the productivity data, and analyzed to produce an intelligence report as illustrated in the Percentage of Overtime Hours Worked by Area chart.

PERCENTAGE OF PRODUCTIVE HOURS WORKED
BY AREA

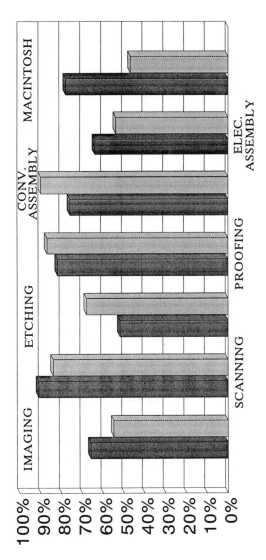

Chart provided by Pat Ternan, Director of Information Management at Color Service, Inc. of Seattle.

PERCENTAGE OF OVERTIME HOURS WORKED
BY AREA

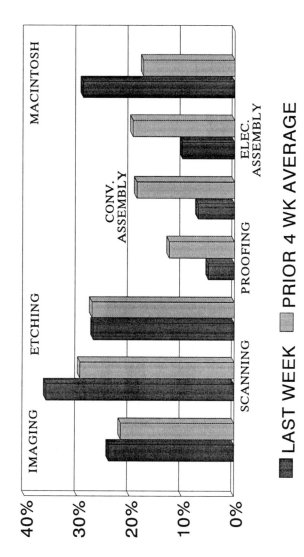

■ LAST WEEK ■ PRIOR 4 WK AVERAGE

Chart provided by Pat Ternan, Director of Information Management at Color Service, Inc. of Seattle.

With these two sets of graphs, an analysis can be accomplished. Several questions should be asked. Is the percent of overtime in sync with the productivity levels? For example, if productivity in a department is only 60 percent and overtime is 20 percent, it is almost always a red flag. Are there significant differences in productivity between departments? Could the Job Engineer redirect work to those departments with low productivity while at the same time avoiding potential production bottlenecks in departments with high productivity?

The intelligence report can also be used to optimize department staffing and determine if hiring or layoffs are necessary. Most nonproductivity is caused by idle time. The worker simply does not have a job to do.

The third key statistic is rework. Defining rework, documenting it through the production process, and measuring its impact on profitability is a difficult challenge. Often, the methodology is driven by the type of automation system and the willingness of the employees to participate in recording rework accurately, completely, and on a timely basis (see Chapter 10, Managing the Process).

One of the most successful ways to document rework is through an employee comment system. Comment codes can be developed for each department, describing the common rework problems pertinent to that portion of the job process flow.

Rework comments can be collected in an automated system or a manual one. In either case, the data must be aggregated, analyzed, and displayed to insure it passes the So What Test. An example of rework data for one department is shown in the chart entitled Cause for Rework—Assembly.

Collection of comments is a voluntary system. All employees must be told why the comments are necessary and how they will be used to determine procedures to reduce costs and, in turn, increase profits.

CAUSE FOR REWORK – ASSEMBLY

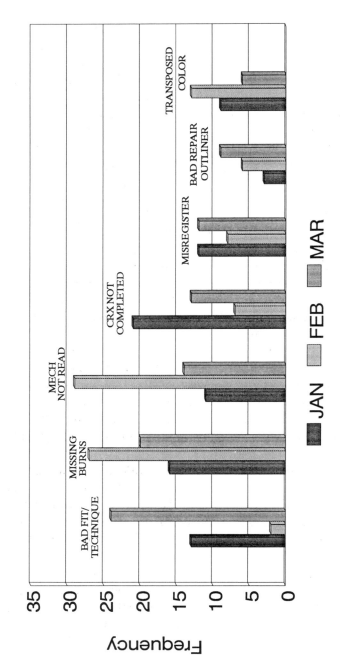

JAN   FEB   MAR

Chart provided by Pat Ternan, Director of Information Management at Color Service, Inc. of Seattle.

Surprising as it may seem, often those departments that produce the most rework comments are doing the best job in reducing rework. If problems are not identified, no solution will be forthcoming. Focusing statistical process control on productivity, overtime, and rework is a good place to start. These data displays can easily pass the So What Test, provided the information is depicted in easy-to-read graphs and accompanied by some analysis of what the results mean to profitability. Other statistical process control measures can be implemented in almost every department. Customer Service can track on-time performance for all jobs, to include the reason(s) jobs are late. Sales can track the direct margin percentage or profit/hour by account, by job, and by sales person. The stripping manager can track material use and waste. Accounting can track days sales outstanding (DSO). The list is endless.

The key to using statistical process control measurement techniques is to start with simple data displays and build toward more complexity, insuring that the So What Test is passed at each step along the way. Once data is assembled, *it must be analyzed.* The final result is an intelligence report that specifically addresses the needs of the president and his management team.

Chapter 8

Marketing

There is not a single subject that is more misunderstood than marketing. For most people marketing and sales are the same thing. They are not. *Marketing* is the science of identification of "who" and "what" and *sales* is the art of "how."

Marketing people are generally not sales types and vice versa. Marketing requires an abundance of information and a lot of analysis. The big value of marketing is it heads a company in the right direction towards *who* it should be doing business with and *what* it should be supplying to the market.

The graphic arts market today is comprised primarily of companies who would be classified as product driven. A product driven company is noted by its orientation to create products and then find a market in which to sell them. A product driven company will first identify the products it thinks it can build better than the competition, commit the resources to build the products, develop sales campaigns to go sell the products, and attempt to secure customers.

This is contrasted by a company that is market driven where the needs of the market are first identified, profitable products are designed to meet those needs, the customers that could use the product are identified, the profit opportunity computed for that market, a decision is made to enter the market, the resources are committed to build the products for that market, the products are built, and the customers are targeted and secured.

The chart entitled Product Versus Market Driven displays a side-by-side comparison of a product driven company and a market driven company.

PRODUCT VERSUS MARKET

MARKET DRIVEN

Research Needs
The company goes to the market and finds the needs of various market segments

Market Segment Selection
The company chooses the market with the best profit potential

Designs Product to Meet Need
The company designs products to meet needs in market segment (Engineering)

Purchases Resources to Build Product
The company acquires the correct resource to build the product

Manufactures Product to Design
The company builds the products to meet the need according to the design

Product Delivery
The company delivers the right product to the right market segment for the right price

PRODUCT DRIVEN

Research Resources
The company researches the state of the art equipment for productivity

Resources Are Selected
The company selects the resources it feels gives it a competitive advantage

Sales Plans are Formed
The company tries to identify customers that will buy the products

Manufactures Products From Sales
The company builds the products based on sales

Product Delivery
The company delivers the products

A frequent question asked in our seminars is, "How do you identify good market segments from poor market segments?" The number one way to differentiate markets is through profitability. In other words, those markets that yield the highest profits are the best markets. The only question is how "highest profits" are to be measured.

Assume the following two jobs need to be prepared:

Job Number	Sales Price	Direct Costs	Direct Margin	Margin Percent
Job #1	$5,000	$2,500	$2,500	50%
Job #2	$5,000	$2,500	$2,500	50%

Without knowing anything but what is shown above, the only thing that can be said about these jobs is that they are equivalent. In this case it would not matter if the company developed the market where it found Job #1 or the market where it found Job #2.

Add some additional information to see if the answer changes:

Job Number	Sales Price	Direct Costs	Direct Margin	Margin Percent	Hours Used
Job #1	$5,000	$2,500	$2,500	50%	10
Job #2	$5,000	$2,500	$2,500	50%	20

The conclusion changes. No longer are these jobs equivalent; Job #1 has a greater throughput than Job #2. If job performance is computed, the following results are obtained.

Job Number	Sales Price	Direct Costs	Direct Margin	Margin %	Hours Used	Profit/ Hour
Job #1	$5,000	$2,500	$2,500	50%	10	$250
Job #2	$5,000	$2,500	$2,500	50%	20	$125

Analyzing the jobs by using a throughput performance measurement, which expresses jobs in terms of profit dollars per hour, it becomes clear that the jobs are no longer equivalent.

Job #	Plant Hrs Capacity	# Jobs Possible	Total Revenue	Total Cost	Total Profit
Job #1	1,000	100	$500,000	$250,000	$250,000
Job #2	1,000	50	$250,000	$125,000	$125,000

The standard analysis performed in this industry is margin analysis as described in the first job scenario above. The problem with using margin analysis is it fails to resolve the problems of decreasing prices, increasing costs, and limited capacities.

The analysis using profit dollars per hour not only takes into account the revenues, costs, and profits of a job, but it also clearly looks at the ability of the job to move quickly through the company utilizing less limited resources and allowing the company to do more jobs in the same given period of time.

What Does This All Mean?

Marketing is really the study of populations. In this case the goal is to identify the most profitable populations in which the company wants to do work. A marketing plan is simply a road map designed to help the company identify the markets and products it would like to sell to a particular group of customers.

Marketing is when a company evaluates the market, selects those segments they want to penetrate, and develops specific sales plans to get the business. Companies that evaluate market segments based on profit dollars per hour will have the edge.

There are various ways to go about evaluating profitable market segments. The easiest way is to specifically describe the components of each segment, find jobs in the market that match up with the component breakdown, and perform profit per dollar estimating on those jobs. If done on a statistical basis, some very good conclusions can be made about those segments.

Company officials often ask why we spend so much time talking about marketing and helping companies in the marketing area.

The answer is quite simple. This industry has excess capacity, there is not enough work to go around, and clients are at war with their competitors. Someone is going to starve.

They also ask about the "great fallout" that everyone thinks will take place over the next couple of years in this industry. Literature available leans toward new technology as the key ingredient to the fallout. The companies who gather the newest STUFF and use it will win. (See Chapter 4, Production STUFF.) This may be a contributor to the fallout, but it will not cause the fallout.

Every industry follows a life cycle. The following chart shows a typical Industry Life Cycle. It is made up of four phases: innovation, growth, maturation, and decline.

INDUSTRY LIFE CYCLE

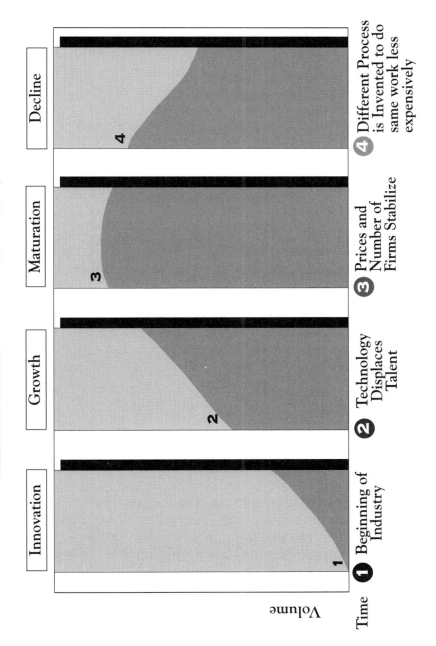

| Innovation | Growth | Maturation | Decline |

Time

Volume

1 Beginning of Industry

2 Technology Displaces Talent

3 Prices and Number of Firms Stabilize

4 Different Process is Invented to do same work less expensively

Industry Life Cycle

Innovation

This phase is the industry's start-up phase. The skilled talent in the industry makes it possible for the industry to operate. Initially, those companies in the marketplace that have gathered or trained the talent and can do the work generally make good profits. Turnaround times are simply limited to the number of skilled people doing the work. Economies of scale have not yet become a reality and the quality issues are substantial and strictly related to the skill of workers.

Growth

This phase is when technology starts to significantly displace talent and economies of scale become a way of life. In the graphic arts industry, there is a breakdown in the borders between different tasks such as design, typography, pre-press, press, bindery, and fulfillment. Quality becomes a given and there becomes a great deal of pressure on turnaround time. There is a tremendous reshuffling of the client bases, business skills start to become much more important, margins are shrinking, and companies must become more efficient. It is this phase of an industry life cycle that generally decides who will be the long-term players.

Maturation

This phase is when technology does not have such a significant impact on the efficiency or effectiveness of the industry. Turnaround times are just about as low as they can go, prices become more stable, and the number of firms has become relatively constant. Maturation takes place after industry fallouts and entrance to the marketplace is not so attractive because the profits in the market are there, but only to those who have substantially created the internal structures to capture those profits. Entrance to the market cannot be made simply by the introduction of more technology.

Decline

This phase is when a completely new method of production of the same products is developed. The new technology can either be introduced through the same suppliers of the old technology or from a completely different source. Whether the same companies will be the ones to adopt the new method will be completely dependent on the nature of the new methods. When a market is in decline, the really efficient companies will be the beneficiary of the decline. Typically, the number of firms decrease rapidly because of the cash situation and the supply temporarily dips. This allows prices to elevate over a very short time period as customers still require goods and services, but the demand exceeds supply. Companies with superior marketing skills will really dominate this phase. For example, this is the phase in which typographers find themselves.

The graphic arts industry is in the growth phase. Developing an internal production engine is essential, but learning how to market is paramount, because market driven companies will be the ones who dominate the growth phase and take wonderful profits during all the confusion.

The "great fallout" will take place over the market share capture. Those companies who build their plans around capturing the type of work that can obtain the highest profit dollars per hour will be the winners. Profit dollars per hour represents the purest form of performance measurement because it divides two absolutes by each other and links profitability to throughput.

Companies will need to revise the way they collect information in order to obtain profit dollars per hour, but it will be well worth it. They will need to build marketing plans in terms of profit dollars per hour. These plans will first come from examining jobs they currently do and jobs they would like to do in terms of profit dollars per hour. As they get more and more comfortable with profit dollars per hour, they will move more rapidly into examining other markets in the same manner and selecting the type of work that yields the best results.

Chapter 9

The Money-Making Formula

MBAs and CPAs will simply say that the Money-Making Formula (MMF) is an income statement depicted graphically. They are right, it is. (See schematic.)

Why is the MMF so powerful? The MMF brings a company back to basics. It refocuses on what really must happen in order for a company to grow. It does not get a company confused with all this accounting Mumbo Jumbo and it describes cleanly and precisely what a company must do to make money.

Using the Money-Making Formula

The following describes the use of a MMF. First, the President should have a "blow up" made and mounted on his wall. He then should have "hand held" models made. The hand held models can be an 8-1/2" x 11" copy laminated. The more serious companies also can use the "travel model."

THE "MONEY MAKING" FORMULA

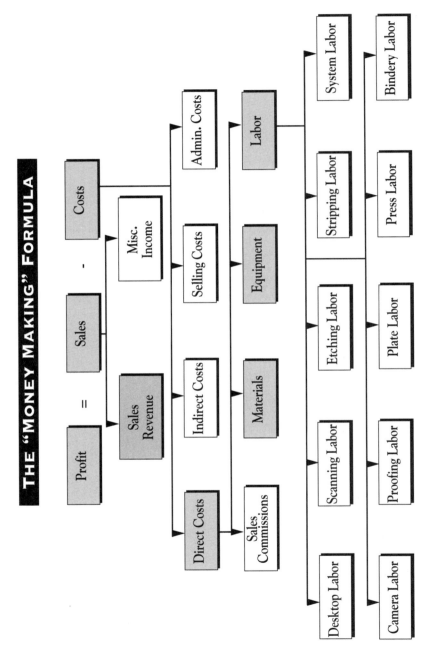

Profit = Sales - Costs

Sales:
- Sales Revenue
- Misc. Income

Costs:
- Direct Costs
- Indirect Costs
- Selling Costs
- Admin. Costs

Direct Costs:
- Sales Commissions
- Materials
- Equipment
- Labor

Labor:
- Desktop Labor
- Scanning Labor
- Etching Labor
- Stripping Labor
- System Labor
- Camera Labor
- Proofing Labor
- Plate Labor
- Press Labor
- Bindery Labor

This is wallet size so their people are never unarmed at Graphic Arts Shows looking at new technology. This is the perfect opportunity to whip out the MMF and ask, "Excuse me, where does this STUFF fit into the MMF?" The silence can be deafening.

The next thing the President can do is explain how all the company meetings must be related to using the MMF. The number of meetings may decrease and even become shorter. The President should insist on only one rule: If you do not come to the meeting with the MMF, do not come.

Inside the meeting, amazing things can happen. Everyone has an equal right to ask the question, "Excuse me, where does your idea or actions fit into the MMF?" The MMF empowers the people and it is the best means of dealing with the "conflict of agreement," better known as the *Abilene Paradox.*

Jerry Harvey wrote a book called the *Abilene Paradox.* It is recommended reading for those who would like to understand the dynamics of the conflict of agreement. The Abilene Paradox goes something like this:

A family living in Coleman, Texas, was just sitting around one Sunday morning not really doing a lot, just sort of relaxing. The father soon offered the suggestion, "Why don't we drive into Abilene today and eat at the diner?" Although he really would have been content just to stay home and read the news-paper, he felt it his fatherly duty to suggest something for the family to do on Sunday.

No one in the family immediately picked up on the idea of driving to Abilene since it was 56 miles from Coleman, it was 100 degrees outside, and the car did not have air conditioning. But soon the son said, "That's not a bad idea, Dad. I will go with you," thinking all along that he did not really want to go to Abilene, but if his Dad really wanted to go, he would go with him.

Next, the son's wife thought, Abilene. You have got to be crazy, but if she was going to be a loyal wife she should support her husband and she then said, "I haven't been to Abilene in years, and if you are going to go, honey, I'll go with you." The sister, thinking she did not want to stay behind alone said, "I guess I will go. There is nothing to do here."

Finally, the whole family went into the kitchen to confront Mother and told her they were all going to Abilene. She said, "Well, if everyone is going, who am I to stand in the way of a family outing," and they all piled into the unairconditioned car, drove 56 miles through the heat and dust, and went to Abilene to have perhaps the worst meal they had ever eaten.

That evening, after they had returned, the son said, "I guess that wasn't so bad," and it was at that point the sister said, "Bad. It was horrible and you are to blame." "Me!" he exclaimed, "I didn't even want to go to Abilene; I only went because Dad wanted to go." Dad responded, "I didn't really want to go; I would have rather just read the paper and relaxed. I just threw out the idea because everyone looked bored. I really didn't even want to go."

It suddenly dawned on the family they had driven a total of 112 miles in the heat and dust, ate horrible food, had a horrible time, and no one really wanted to go.

The Abilene Paradox, the conflict of agreement, had taken place. Many times a person finds himself in political environments faced with the acceptance of ideas he does not really support, but after weighing the consequences of disagreeing, he agrees, hoping the blame can at least be shouldered or lost within the group structure.

The MMF, if applied properly, prevents things like the Abilene Paradox from occurring. It also works exactly the same in the *conflict of disagreement*. If the ownership or upper management provides the company the power of the MMF, it then becomes the basis of conflict resolution, whether the conflict arises out of agreement or disagreement.

Funny things happen inside companies that adopt the MMF. Everyone becomes aware of the MMF. Production flows, budgets, marketing plans, acquisitions of STUFF, and performance bonuses all start to take on a new meaning and get implemented differently. The company starts to transform and get more competitive.

People start to apply what is called the *Pencil Theory*, which is described as follows: If an employee was in the back of the plant and accidentally broke his pencil and asked to purchase a new one, it would immediately decrease the profit of the company, unless a corresponding amount of sales could be made at a profit to cover the cost of the pencil. It is that simple and it is that dramatic. Do not let all the costs get shoved over into little accounting boxes with explanations. Ask the MMF questions about everything.

Chapter 10

Managing the Process

Edwards W. Deming, the architect of the quality revolution in Japan, often has been quoted that 85 percent of all defects and rework in a plant can be attributed directly to faulty processes and only 15 percent directly to the employees. Our studies of a number of companies in the graphic arts industry have documented similar findings.

What is a process? First, it is not an office manual on policies and procedures. Second, it is not a job description for a particular workstation. Third, it is not how a company would like jobs to flow through the plant.

A process is a detailed work flow layout of all the paths jobs can travel from the "front door" to the "back door." A description of work flows is essential in order to have a base line to improve the process. The location of the bottlenecks, delays, under and over capacity, and the sources of rework will not be identified fully unless the entire process is examined from start to finish.

What one department supervisor perceives as a production bottleneck may not be the root cause of the problem at all. For example, in one company we repeatedly heard that the problem limiting throughput was the Macintosh department. They just did not know how to process the jobs arriving from clients on diskettes.

On careful analysis we discovered that the real problem was a much broader one, centering on a lack of communication between the clients, Mac operators, and the high-end electronic system operators who received the files from the Macs. Neither group of workers had a clear understanding of the other's needs or how the client had built the page.

The first step in performing a complete work flow layout is to diagram the front-end planning system. (See Chapter 3, Front-end Planning.) This portion of the work flow should take the job from the client into the production department and be standardized for all jobs.

The Job Engineer and Production Manager should then diagram the major alternative work flows for different types of jobs. These can include conventional work flows; electronic work flows with or without client prepared diskettes for line work; various service bureau functions such as plotting film from diskettes; and different printing processes.

In a small conventional company, there should be at least two or three basic work flows. In mid-sized companies with a mix of conventional and electronic systems, or multiple presses, there can be eight or nine work flows, each with variants.

Each functional area (e.g., scanning, stripping, dot etching, electronic page assembly, press, bindery) should be identified on the work paths. The job approval and billing functions should be added at the "back end" of the work flows.

When completed, the work flows become an organization chart for the company. The function and interrelationship of every employee in the plant can now be displayed on one or more of the work flows.

Once the work flows have been carefully documented, potential rework loops should be penciled in for each work flow. A rework loop occurs when a job starts at a point in the process, continues through one or more production functions, and then is returned to the starting point because of rework at one or more points along the way.

The next step is to document the actual points in the work flow where the need for rework is first identified. Often this will be at the end of one or more sequential rework loops, as opposed to at an early stage in the process. In many companies, rework is not identified until the job reaches the customer service or sales representative, or even worse, the client.

When most rework is identified only at the end of the production process, such as by the CSR, it suggests an endemic quality problem within the plant. Quality is in fact being controlled by what Dr. Edwards W. Deming calls *mass inspection*. Other names such as Quality Control (QC) Manager also could be used.

Controlling quality at the end of the process can have a very negative effect on the company. First, it relieves individual employees of the responsibility for building quality into his or her own work. And second, it insures a high cost in time, labor, materials, and machines to rework the job. The profit margin can drop dramatically. The net result might look like this:

	QUOTE	ACTUAL
Job Price	$1,000	$1,000
Labor	210	360
Materials	130	170
Machine	95	160
Commission	100	100

Direct Costs	535	790
Direct Margin	465	210
Direct Margin %	46.5%	21.0%

If the indirect, selling, and administrative costs (see Chapter 5, Direct Costing and Labor) are 41 percent, it means the company fell 20 percent short of covering overhead costs.

One approach to reducing rework is to move the responsibilities for quality to every employee in the company. Yes, every employee in the company! Employees are the best source to determine the root causes of rework and come up with positive, common sense solutions to these problems.

In order to transform the company from mass inspection at the end of the production cycle to quality throughout the process, a new attitude needs to be developed. This change must begin with the President and his upper management team.

A commitment to the quality transformation process needs to be more than lip service. Employees often will tell us how their company starts one "new" program only to stop or let it die a few weeks later. Employees are as leery of new programs as a cutthroat trout is of a fly fisherman walking with a golden retriever on the shores of a high mountain lake.

A seminar with the top management is an excellent way to discuss what commitment to quality really means. These seminars require a day or so and should be conducted in an atmosphere away from the hour-to-hour "crises" in the plant. The theme for the seminar is *managing the process*," not managing jobs or employees. Outside assistance almost always is required in order to help everyone "see the forest through the trees.''

Inherent in this transformation to a process oriented management system is the delegation of a good deal more authority to each worker. All employees must be encouraged to identify and report the occurrence and root causes of rework, to include "turning themselves in" for problems at their workstation or in their department. The success depends on the level of participation and commitment to quality.

To create this new corporate culture, employees must be certain that the management will listen to them and that they will not be penalized with a missed promotion or reduced pay raise for this type of open and honest communication.

Once the long-term commitment of management is received, it is time to select a small group of key employees, the Transformation Team, to guide the process.

In a small- to mid-sized company, the Transformation Team should consist of a maximum of a dozen employees. These should include selected department heads and experienced employees from *every* department. All shifts should be represented, but as a minimum, employees from the day and evening shifts need to be in attendance. This normally will lead to meetings being held at shift change. Overtime should not be paid for these meetings.

After working with a number of graphic arts companies with Transformation Teams, our studies reflect that things get off to a fast start only to bog down after a few weeks. The two key reasons are a lack of focus on rework and failure of the upper management to insist that the team meetings be held regularly and frequently (every other week or at least monthly).

Rework should be the focus. Rework is bad. Rework is nonpersonal. Rework steals profits from the company. Rework is a company disease. Everyone knows it is present. Most people want to cure the disease. If rework is reduced, *most other problems are solved at the same time.* Rework can only be reduced by documenting what causes the problems (see Chapter 7, Statistical Process Control). The Transformation Team needs to be chaired by a person who is very comfortable with small group mechanics and organizational issues. He or she must draft detailed agendas for the meetings, keep the discussions keyed to the agenda items, create an atmosphere where people want to discuss problems and solutions, and document the minutes of the meetings for *all* employees to read.

In addition to the standing members of the Transformation Team, other employees should be invited to attend as observers. Perhaps two or three observers can attend each meeting. They should be offered a few minutes to provide their observations on how the process can be improved.

The role of the President and upper management in regard to the Transformation Team is a delicate one. We believe that owners and senior managers probably should not be members of the Transformation Team. Despite what they may believe, owners do intimidate employees to one degree or another. If owners wish to attend the meetings, and in many cases they should, it is important that they attend as observers.

The critical role of the owner is to work behind the scenes to insure the Transformation Team meetings are held on a regular basis, that the agendas are prepared and distributed in advance, and that the meetings are productive. If the discussions begin to drift to areas that are outside the scope of the Transformation Team, then the owner can take the team chairman aside and provide the necessary guidance to refocus the meetings.

The President and the upper management team set the stage for the Transformation Team to be successful in improving the process. Delegation of authority to accomplish the transformation is important. It does not mean, however, that the management team is no longer running the company.

There is a difference between managing the process and managing the company. There are strategic issues that must be addressed by the senior management team that go well beyond the scope of the Transformation Team. These include marketing, cash flow, hiring/firing/layoffs, capital acquisitions, mergers, and environmental-related work issues such as shift hours and dress codes.

On balance, the President must become much more pro-active and lead the company to profitability. He or she should demand good job related information and projections from sales, finance, the management information system, and production. With these tools, the President can adopt and measure the effects of a process oriented management system involving every employee in the company. Productivity will improve, rework will drop, and customer satisfaction will be enhanced. The President will see the forest—despite all the trees!

Gary Millet (left) and Ralph Rosenberg
at Gary and Maria's wedding.

Epilogue

Making money certainly presents it challenges. You do not have lots of time to try to figure it out. The challenges facing us today are completely different from the challenges of the past and they require different skills to be successful.

There is not a single company or person who has all the answers. The answers you do need, however, must lead you and your company to improving profits, because over the long term only profitable companies survive. In the short term, *watch your cash.*

We have enjoyed putting together this primer and even more in helping our clients implement these ideas. It is our current assessment of the industry. Hopefully, it will be used as a desktop reference book that can help provide a few of the answers you need, guide you and your company to greater profits, and help reduce a little stress in your life.

We wish everyone good luck in meeting the new challenges and finding their opportunities to succeed.

Profile of Millet Group, Inc.

Millet Group, Inc., specializes in business and production consulting to the graphic arts industry and other industries using job process flow manufacturing. Products and services include equipment configuration and return on investment analyses; the design and implementation of cost effective production processes and work flows; creation of marketing and sales plans; presentation of sales training seminars; conversion of companies to a total quality management system; preparation of growth models to integrate new technology into all aspects of company operations; and benchmark testing of new equipment technologies and configurations.

The corporation maintains four regional offices to service its nationwide client base. These offices are in Paramus, New Jersey; Chicago, Illinois; Atlanta, Georgia; and Los Angeles, California.

Gary W. Millet, President of Millet Group, Inc., entered the graphic arts industry 10 years ago as co-founder of a management information systems software company designed to provide a full range of data collection and information reports to pre-press and printing companies. During this period he was frequently asked to provide consulting services as an extension of his hardware and software needs analysis to client companies. In response to increased consulting demands by these companies, and new clients, Gary formed the Millet Group in 1990 in order to devote all of his efforts to consulting focused on increasing client profitability. Gary earned an MBA from the University of Utah in 1976 and became a Certified Public Accountant in 1978.

Ralph G. Rosenberg, Vice President and General Manager of Millet Group, spent over 10 years in operations research/ systems analysis positions after obtaining a Master of Science in Systems Management from the University of Southern California in 1973. He gained hands-on, small business expertise as the owner and general manager of a progressive retail company. Following its successful sale in 1988, he began consulting with the Millet Group. Ralph specializes in graphic arts business analysis, total quality management, statistical process control, and equipment benchmark testing in support of research and development. In 1993 Ralph earned his Certified Management Consultant (CMC) designation.

For more information on the Millet Group, to order a copy of this book ($14.95 USD plus $3.00 shipping), or to order our video on the "Millet Triangle" ($29.95 USD plus $3.00 shipping), please contact:

△ **Millet Group, Inc.**
5012 Cliff Point Circle West
Colorado Springs, CO 80919
Telephone: (719) 531-0669
FAX: (719) 592-9081

Give the Money-Making Formula for Graphic Arts to Your Friends and Colleagues!

ORDER FORM

YES, I want ____ copies of *Primer for Graphic Arts Profitability* at $14.95 USD each, plus $3 shipping per book. (No credit cards, please.) Allow 5 days for delivery.

☐ My check for $ _____ is enclosed.
☐ Please invoice me for the purchase.

Name _____ Phone _____

Company _____

Address _____

City/State/Zip _____

Please mail or fax your order to:

△ **Millet Group, Inc.**
5012 Cliff Point Circle West
Colorado Springs, CO 80919
TEL: 719-531-0669
FAX: 719-592-9081

Order the "Millet Triangle" Video

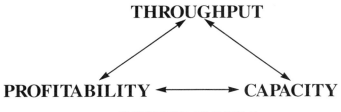

ORDER FORM

This eight-minute video is an excerpt from a seminar given by Gary Millet, President of Millet Group, on the Millet Triangle. It shows the interrelationships between job throughput, plant capacity and company profitability. The key variables in this analysis are definition of work flows, examination of the cost of the speed of the configurations, and profitability, as determined by sales less operating costs. Allow 5 days for delivery.

YES, I want ____copies of the "Millet Triangle" video at $29.95 USD each, plus $3 shipping. (No credit cards, please.)

☐ My check for $ _____ is enclosed.
☐ Please invoice me for the purchase.

Name _____ Phone _____

Company _____

Address _____

City/State/Zip _____

Please mail or fax your order to:

△ **Millet Group, Inc.**
5012 Cliff Point Circle West
Colorado Springs, CO 80919
TEL: 719-531-0669
FAX: 719-592-9081

© 1993 Millet Group, Inc.